By David Meltzer

POETRY

Poems (w/ Donald Schenker)
(1957)
Ragas (1959)
The Clown (1960)
The Process (1965)
The Dark Continent (1967)
Round the Poem Box (1969)
Yesod (1969)
From Eden Book (1969)
Greenspeech (1970)
Luna (1970)
Knots (1971)
Bark (1973)
Tens, Selected Poems:
1961–71 (1973)
Hero/Lil (1973)
The Eyes, the Blood (1973)
Blue Rags (1974)
Harps (1975)
Six (1976)
The Art, the Veil (1981)
Arrows: Selected Poetry
1957–1992 (1994)
No Eyes: Lester Young (2000)

CHILDREN'S TALES

Abra (illustrated by John
Brandi) (1976)

FICTION

The Agent (1968)
The Agency (1968)
How Many Blocks in the Pile?
(1969)
Orf (1969)
The Martyr (1969)
Lovely (1969)
Healer (1969)
Out (1969)
Glue Factory (1969)
Star (1970)

ESSAYS

We All Have Something to Say
to Each Other:
An Essay on Kenneth
Patchen (1962)
Bazascope Mother (on Robert
Alexander) (1964)
Journal of the Birth (1967)
Isla Vista Notes (1970)
Two-Way Mirror: A Poetry
Notebook (1977)

TRANSLATION

Morning Glories by Shiga
Naoya (in collaboration
with Allen Say) (1976)

ANTHOLOGIES

The San Francisco Poets (1971)
Golden Gate: Interviews with Five San Francisco Poets (1976)
The Secret Garden: Anthology of the Classical Kabbalah
(1976)
The Path of the Names: Writings by Abraham ben Samuel
Abulafia (1976)
Birth: An Anthology of Ancient Texts, Songs, Prayers, and
Stories (1981)
Death: An Anthology of Texts, Songs, Charms, Prayers, and
Stories (1984)

DAVID MELTZER

NO EYES: LESTER YOUNG

BLACK SPARROW PRESS • SANTA ROSA • 2000

No Eyes: Lester Young. Copyright © 2000 by David Meltzer.

The author and publisher would like to thank the Ray Avery Jazz Archives for the photographs used in this book.

Black Sparrow Press books are printed on acid-free paper.

LIBRARY OF CONGRESS CATALOGING-IN-PUBLICATION DATA

Meltzer, David
   No Eyes : Lester Young / David Meltzer
     p.   cm.
   ISBN 1-57423-129-4 (paperback)
   ISBN 1-57423-130-8 (cloth trade)
   ISBN 1-57423-131-6 (signed cloth)
     1. Young, Lester, 1909–1959—Poetry. 2. Jazz musicians—
Poetry. 3. Jazz—Poetry. I. Title.
   PS3563.E45 N6 2000
   811'.54—dc21   00-36101

To the fallen and the arising
To ever abiding Aya
To Lew

This sequence of poems is a prolonged meditation on the last year of Lester Young's life. It was inspired by a newspaper photo in the Sunday *New York Times Book Review* section in the early '60s: Young sits on his bed in the Arvin Hotel in Manhattan the year before he died. Ghastly pale, stooped, he holds his tenor saxophone in his lap, his right hand covers its bell. The bed's made but somehow rumpled; there's a phone on the small night table by the bed & the hooded nozzle of the tenor's leather carrying case. Everything in the picture seems to slant downward. I've carried the photograph with me for decades. It's on yellowed & wrinkled newsprint stock giving it a talismanic aura.

The facts: Lester Willis Young was born in Woodville, Mississippi on August 27th 1909 and died in the Arvin Hotel in Manhattan March 15th 1959. He came from a musical family. His father was a trained musician who studied at Tuskegee, who instructed Young on trumpet, violin, alto sax & drums.

He came to prominence as part of the Count Basie Band during the late '30s and early '40s. His studio sessions for Columbia with Billie Holiday remain quintessential as do his Commodore recordings with the Kansas City Six and Seven. He was drafted into the Army during WW2 and brigged for narcotics and courtmartialled which many say permanently damaged his immensely sensitive emotional equilibrium.

≀

Lester Young and Coleman Hawkins were the major pathways for jazz tenor players to explore their art through. Hawkins projected a deep and full aggressive attack rooted in a sophisticated "modern" harmonic sensibility. Young was a lyrical player, shaping solos into complete compositions; his tone was light and airy, inevitably haunted by breathy melancholy. Hawkins swung hard, Young swung lightly though not politely. Both men had a major influence on Bebop players as well as subsequent historically inevitable jazz eruptions.

≀

Young's style predates and anticipates the post-bop "cool" jazz. Yet "cool jazz" in its moment was criticized as being unemotional and too cerebral, whereas any solo by Young was always deeply felt even when sounding casual. If Hawkins was overt in his forceful display of chops and fire, Young was insinuatingly covert. Young was a lover, a seducer, a romancer, a broken heart mending the world in so many bars of a chorus.

≀

Barely legal in Hollywood—exiled from Brooklyn—I luckily fell in with a distinctly eclectic cadre of disaffiliates, margin magi, whose splendid disruptive company included many jazz musicians. Paul and

Carla Bley had a flat above a gas station in Hollywood on Santa Monica Boulevard where young and seasoned musicians came at night to play until morning. Met many players including Warne Marsh, whose work with Lee Konitz and Lennie Tristano were as central to my musical self as Parker and Monk.

As the mythopoem goes, Bird crafted his art by slowing down Young's solos to learn them and then play them double or triple time. Prez was the root and Yard the branch.

The most noted sax playing Tristanoites were Lee Konitz and Warne Marsh, whose training (ear and voice) required that they replicate vocally and then instrumentally solos by Parker, Young, as well as Bach. Get the song in the ear, your voice, breath, then through the brass air chamber and keypads of the horn. Young insisted that you had to know the melody of a song as well as its lyrics. Words were as important to Prez as melody. A poet in the fullest sense, Young inspired generations of players, gave them permission to follow the lyric mode, the deep cool as differentiated from the shallow cool of costume and surface. Some of his earliest and foremost disciples were Stan Getz, Don Byas, Serge Chaloff, Paul Quinichette, Zoot Sims.

≀

Today, then, is the day
the melting snowman
is a real man.

wrote Japanese haiku poet Fusen in 1777, the year he died at age 57. Lester Young died at 50. Some say of a broken heart, others of a damaged spirit, others speak of racism, others of being a poet in a country which finds poetry impossible, others of having reached song's end.

> *Arriving, all is clear, no doubt about it.*
> *Going, all is clear, without a doubt.*
> *What, then, is it all about?*

wrote 13th century Zen monk Hosshin before death.

≀

What, then, does "no eyes" or "eyes" mean? At core: to see or not see, to be or not to be. With it or against it. In hipster parlance, "no eyes" lets a lot of stipple shadow-splatter the divide. Diffident: —I have no eyes to go to Costco. Defiant: —I have no eyes for politics or (as a variant) for belief systematized or loosely dogmatic. Deliberate: —I have no eyes for your paradiddle. Demanding: —I have no eyes for your paradise.

You get the drift. To have "eyes" riffs out easily enough: —Eyes to groove to the grave; eyes to burrow between your thighs; eyes to thrive, no jive; eyes to see, be. All the cornball clichés including "seeing the light" work for me.

≀

In recordings where Young is in small group settings you are inside a dialogic delicacy and spaciousness contrary to the big band heavy thunder of the era.

Count Basie's minimal maximum swing connotations and propulsions, Jo Jones's firm but delicate insistent drums, Walter Page on bass, Freddie Green's discreet rhythm guitar, created a dream cloud for Young to compose recompositions of familiar songs and blues riffs. Prez adhered to that economy of creation for the rest of his career. Like his direct protégé Charlie Parker, Young rarely took more than three or four choruses of improvisation in any number, and like Parker he stayed within a basic repertoire of show tunes, pop songs, and blues.

All who knew him testify to his sensitivity and unique trickster hipster masking of language to code his relationship to the world of crunch and edge.

Affirmation through creation and destruction play their contradictions like chord changes. How a life refuses itself yet recreates itself on the bandstand unhesitatingly but sits afterwards for days in a hotel room waiting to die without noticing it. How does such a presence practice such absencing?

𝄩

The metaphor of creation and negation, of despair's art and the art of melancholy, haunt this poem. It's about death and Young sits in as a metaphor for an imaginary (yet acknowledgeably great) artist living and dying for and with his art.

𝄩

1:iv:00

NO EYES: LESTER YOUNG

Lester had "no eyes" for bad vibes crude moves
abrasive invasive uncool imposition on smooth flow
create sounds through smoke-filled black and white

Lester's retreat was away from injury
at times light was knives, her softness
his desire for flight

No eyes for hassle
brute verbal confrontation
rage fists knee gut slam jolt
to settle a linguistic entanglement
prefer a distancing reverie
easy fold into fold of sound against soul
cashmere

Defeat cap in mud
knocked off head
papa cowers from thug
won't protect son
from violence

You're in the Army now
a little Jew guy sings on stage in a movie
O how I hate to get up in the morning
Lester in the exile brig gig

cops a plea yes sir no sir

No eyes for disdain
pain of face of skin of race

No eyes to smash brains into cellophane
no eyes for paradise if it's ruled & regular

no eyes for outsize posters
no eyes to chew chump food on the q.t.
beauty not nourishment

no eyes for intrusion or delusion
no eyes for skin confusion
no eyes for diffused blues
no eyes no eyes

but eyes for guys who play sympathy changes
no symphonies
listen to my news
dues is truth
deep eyes for struggle
for flight
no eyes for escape

⌒

eyes size up every detail
seize silk curve skin delirium
dig impossibility as plausibility
eyes move through
you know how it goes
hydromatic fluid-drive eyes
click into gear & go

eyes to groove for the lamest cat
blowing pure heart
into clouds of shinola
ah eyes

no eyes for uncool paradise
too much like reading
no eyes for anything but paradox twist
no eyes but sighs
breath through brass insides
a new funky joint
turns your head beyond reach
teach stuck locked shoes
breathe unblock
breaks me up
eyes for that
for freedom wherever it lands

eyes for a level spread
always arising equal anew
no eyes for dragsters dumbsters dullsters
no eyes for cruel rules numbhead owners
managers manipulators regurgitators chronic agitators
no eyes no eyes
eyes for sky pure intent regardless
eyes for deep heart O milky silk
no eyes for no
yes yes
no more Mr In-Between
eyes to dream
wise eyes to ask when it counts
eyes to work ever generous songs
sighing eyes
once I was blind but now I see
eyes to see

eyes to hear touch taste blues gone
blues of the found instant recirculated
eyes for faraway cool dragon root China
eyes for big rivers carrying nothing but fat moist
perfumey heaps of huge gorgeous flower petals
riverbanks bands play around the world
all of me why not take all of me

eyes for prisoner of love me or leave me
eyes for taking a chance on love is here to stay
eyes for just you just me eyes for Indiana
eyes for all those foolish things that remind me
I can't get started on the sunny side of the street
it's almost like being in love
no eyes is blindness
no eyes is Hamlet skull
in cool Larry O black & white
not to see but hear
to tap tap ridges & edges
of streetcorner solid world
stand there blowing ride cymbal of coins
popped into tin baking cup I cook
my eyes into blue dream stew

ff

the bell eyes ring when you don't swing
no eyes for G.I. jive
the bell eyes ring when you don't swing
no eyes for stockades
no eyes for court martial
no eyes for the skin game
the bell eyes ring when you don't swing
eyes to juice & look across the street at Birdland
hear young cats cut Prez in their dreams
hear young cats cut threads to drape smooth glide
only one of a kind every time I enter the joint
hey Bird with your axe in a paper bag I love you too
eyes for blues whose shoes ties us links us
pulled down from deep mellow unbearable
eyes for blues for love forever

⌒

back home again in smoke & elixirs
astounded & adrift outside looking farther out
you & night & music make a universe
soft as the inner liquid lip of your sex all lit up
as in a sunrise
eyes for that
you dig

you dig how it goes down
we turn out of the slap
breathe in & blow utopia
soaked in cigarette smoke

you dig how it goes
down to a blue cellar
changes
of an infinite
repertoire

you dig how it is & isn't
the same love song
broken into parts of big heart
without doubt

back out the back door man
pelted with blossoms no head imagines

bright coins from old blaze
some lady melts
down into a horn she hands me
you dig

slow lambs lope up & down green cartoon hills
blue into violet satin folds across hips that won't quit
lacquer red lips unpart where white teeth glisten & wait
do you hear
are you listening when sound spirit
passes through stuff you thought made you hip

you dig it's a gig

vibe tones hair conk sizzle
they ask me what I do
a secret from all zones
into simple necessary breathing

is it sauce or reefer
works inside fingers padding notes
brass tunnel lady flower carved sworl
play pretty is as pretty does

do you do right

they ask me how I knew
what I know
how it works
open secrets

☊

blind Homer no eyes sang history
warriors & kids need to know
hot to go into blades seek glory
no eyes for Army
bad scene
G.I. jive you dig
court martial gig you dig
dark cell closed door
weird pad of pain
hurt my soul to sing there
melancholy baby
yes sir no sir
how many miles to Birdland
out the window cats below
jive & shuck & wait to solo
you're known by your solo
your thumbprint out there
in their face in space
ladies one & all
caught in song
you dig
eyes

draped reet pleated jazz
threads flow love song line
web you into blue cocoon
oh mellow down easy gate

glowing show go go go
manly eyes for whys but
slice the dice fate digs out
an unarranged heart
held up to red gel spot
meat lotus unpetals on the offbeat
dig it

cut line garment flow
chain link dazzle raiment
pegged & ankled into pointy suede toe
cool pose finery too hip to sweat
too with it to want it
beyond it above it immaculate

⌢

I look out for every loveliness
pretending is all I do
hide a heart that's blue
when the world's cold
discovered the story was phony

he ain't got rhythm
so no one's with him
the loneliest man in town
lowliest man around
what do I get
what am I giving
not the same as I used to be
tragedy seems the end of me
born to love
hiding a heart that's blue

so blow man blow
ofay crew-cuts puke go go go
Bean states majesty
hip suave garbed in finest finery
bell to bell jump beyond blues
honky college kids
holler for honking

I look out for every loveliness

it's night
arise silk flowers
look out for every loveliness
downstairs unpack their cases
love's already scouting the club

toke herb spiral bells
listen to her sea
my heresy luxury
erase extras

breath eyes of ring bells high
on bed's edge horn case closed
Broadway neon blink blink
hit edge of burning sauce

bells count
push line resolve
in fluid brushed Zildjian cymbals
Jo sizzle amour tour of space
veils float throughout
broken heart thoroughfare
ensembled & assembled into one
solo after another after all hours collapse
into one moment going after another

no eyes to stay empty
hotel window dig night lights move
zigzag streets below
great white way runs me underground
collect sounds in bright pink shells
black platter ghosts wail back from paradise
eyes for paradise above beyond the great white way
eyes for paradox a perfect solo no one knows or hears
eyes drink beyond fear fly home
eyes see through you to you
you dig

no eyes to stay on the great white way
the great khaki way
walk in circles around exercise yard in the brig way
on Broadway where Birdland & Royal Roost
stage ghosts of me
am floored above it look down
I'm drinking not eating
eyes to be a hummingbird
fly away from here

fade away from world weight
fade away snapshot too long in light
fade away sound of last solo
room for spit dew to rust pads & keys
fade away reality truth
fade away as a way away from it all
fade away gold scroll tarnished horn
nobody plays it
lean against shaping force
tilt into it

how did it end
not on Valentine's Day
lost in sways of satin lips
gin perfume whiskey burn

how did it end
not on New Year's Eve
her bouquet popped corks
colored petal flakes
stained glass confetti

how did it end
not between sets
puff bells
jukebox bubbles

how did it end
in the family band
play by ear
refuse to read
but make music make it

who knows
day bit cracks in sky she pours through
who knew
you dig

all of me why not take all of me
can't you see me
no photograph or drawn wrong
album cover
can't you see it was unseen
sound deep inside
corroding meat inside tender sighs
fumbles get slick in one note honks
in impossibly profound breath
why not take all of me
I make air vanish & appear in
smears & glisses without wobble
instead dry clarity of throb
broken heart confetti all of me

takes two to tango two to wrangle
what do you do
solo in dawn's cold shoulder
alone but not waiting
days tangled in riffs
distinct snowflake fingerprint
new song standards
beyond words & never absurd
takes two to tangle
no solo

leaps in urgent & honking
insistent wail cajole
sometimes turn the curl whimper & sigh
jump high moon cats draped in ears & eyes
fearless supple muscles of inspiration
rippling riff heads with unlaced enthusiasm
vast open music awake
enchanted hepcats murmur
& dancers grind satin pelvis
writhe & thrive in wet fur
jive alive in blue serge flip
dig it

born in summer heat August 27th
Virgo a pure soul
nothing's sure but give way to air
despair coiled around brass of blues
who'd know how alone each sound is
chained to surprise
lies your gods nail me
caress me embed me in a heel of light
stomp down supple spine
sip fire's edge
hard soil clay fist open up lone flower
she pins to her hair before walking on stage

minimum to the max jim
you dig
in between what you hear
I'm all over the place
spine sing to thee in shadows
lips part in digging amaze
big eyes for what's at the end of the chorus
rim shot
big eyes for where your hand reaches
out in smoke to pull away dust from sparkle
snowball over cats who stand or
sit on chairs tranced
to dance of light darts thread souls
roll them all out onto a vivid plush carpet
writhing Allah weaves through blaze
blind torch probe past all boundary delight
whew

could pray could stick around to watch
angels glide down
hit the dance floor
do a wishbone split
in zoot moves splendidly pegged
could stay to pray shafts of goldleaf light
crash down on footworn wood boards
gold coins faithful scoop into paperbags
run home buy time a stack of platters
party all weekend
could do this
big eyes to do ordinary
hope once more
could do this
did it once or twice
went home for chicken & kids & pet the mutt
but lost touch in soft sheen of sheer
melody ribbons unspool from brass bell
twist up in her hair coils so cool
around her perfect head & sex filled lips
dig it
in hotelroom reruns
brain flicks click snapshot stops
can't get started
the party's over

no skin inside the song is you
no knives or bayonets get through
no guppy picture taker
soul snatcher watchdog
see how death sculpts our cool away

no hat before your Weegee face
no I.D. to get from place to place
no passport to your heart just you
just me dissolving inside out in a negative

f   ℗   𝅘𝅥𝅯

𝄽

how slow can you go before it stops
into a photograph a memory
of a used-up cat at the ledge at the edge
of a hotelroom bed & a saxophone nearby
everything silent & stopped in black & white
hatless & sad in willed emptiness
taking odds when grim scythe comes to gather him
          away

press down key-pads to funnel breath through a
          brass
tunnel moist hot soundprints roll out slippery mellow
          tones
stoned ears revere in now ever intense & dig
the slowed-down clock evaporate between your ears
ripe fruit gone rancid spills out all over the place

you can almost see ghosts in sound
clouds of breath & smoke
her honey lipstick parts to watch
blue skies roll by overhead
got you under my skin & it's Chinese
Cherokee African Irish impossible
blues slip out the back door tip toe
ghosts surround each sound slowing down

𝄐

one way is to stop eating in between drinking
waste away yet stay wasted
you dig

vanish except in photographs
disappear & reappear on album covers
how to leave but still be in the air
all of me

one way is to stay silent
on the hotelroom bedspread
stoic sauce crunching kidneys & liver
hard as a rubber doorstop

how to stop I can't get started
how to wear cool threads now tight
around guts my legs shrink
skin flakes caught up into dust

sad as dust
old Bill's spaces fill rhythm
gold ride wavelengths
blue boys & girls
slip & slide to
jeepers creepers where didcha get those peepers

just you just me
dreaming as one ah
dreamy Brooklyn nights
ofay blends mulatto tans
booking mix uptown
soldier boy gulps reefer bells
gets ass kicked in the brig
for banging white women
okay am tired of the same old
story how you fall down the hole
hit the bottom & break
they're waiting for the next set

lady this & lady that
I'm the namer the sayer
up 'n' Adam halfway out the garden
chased by a rakey snake slamming the door shut
lady Eve whose day got caught covering up
her ladyness w/ leafy shame

am the namer not the blamer
hip to each word song hangs in air to tell
lady luck runs out w/ the bass player
drummers get nothing but leftovers
their kit's too big to pack in a hurry
I switched to reeds & touch every dot in your heart

lady this & lady that
like royalty I dub thee
loyalty scrubs thee skinless
winners losers bad cat bruisers
name thee lady this & lady that

Adam's spook I speak new riddles
cats scuffle what's he getting at
rats scuttle out of sight
pound your lights out
lady your name is death & love
a riff between the beat

I name like the clay man
what I say it is it is
what it is is what I say
is you is or is you ain't my lady

dig the paper moon full & dangerous white tonight
dig loose wig cats pulled by the tripper
do shit to other cats
cut up air with fast & sharp notes
dig how it all plays out
while I stay out of it upstairs
plop a platter on the phono & dig Jo Stafford
woven up in nylon strings sheer as first wound
wind down in the micro crack between night & day
you are the one in cold gray before warm orange
colored sky opens Broadway up to day people

can't give you anything but love
that's the only thing I've plenty of
baby sweet pea curled up & coiled
already spoiled by skin & love's end
without question or sass
what can I tell you baby
what can I say
all of me
coming into light
all dark blue hurt from that moment on
why was I born to leap into one
note tension touch each button
drove you sublime in release
buffed brass silver plate cornucopia
utopia every second of my solo
so low it soaks into earth heat
mulch ground of round tones
hold your face
in my hands
dig it

♭♭

clear moon slice
what a night for death
streetlight eye pain
berserk neons down Broadway
they stand in doorways coffins
deal & hustle it's all good
& done & I'm still chorusing
naming not blaming
no retreat merely returning

glass star slivers poke glaze dim
near almost there
touch ceiling with a blue brush
paint the room black & shut the door

ways & means of pain but sometimes
announce its work through body & soul
delivers a telegram without asking for tips
like speech we all play music
just another way of making up
the world & self on the spot

those tapdance cats in top hats & tails
tickle elegant clicks on shiny floors
& on Lucite chrome-rimmed tables
free of burden & word entangled rhythms
weep at gates almost open

always a cool dresser in the coolest threads
it's a skin world
you catch it glide over glass windows
where eyes see & say who walks
who gets stopped & who never gets going

we make paradise night after night
you & me on stage inventing
what the world can be
music rearranges possibility
dig it when you're in it
it's not like anything else

whatever they say they never knew me
but through me
knew something only I could give them
will you vamp when I name you at the end
& bend the notes before you're gone & I'm smoke
up the ventilator
the band's blasting
outlasts all comers but I will name you at the end
& you will turn to gleam & swing beyond belief
we all go out kaboom
end riff

slow fog on boo dig every dust speck
makes art instantly clear
melancholy baby
turn away into white silk folds
stolen from above
we name we boost
it's one swift move

free flowing elementals
air & fire & salty tears
awake to art alerts
how long has this been going on

protect life advance sound
instant music & after words
man we sit there stunned
when song's gone
nada to say

riff elope out there beyond hooks
skin or gin
let go released
given away

like a spiritual

let my people go
down to get you in a
taxi honey all of me

in boxer shorts a water glass
of gin hooker lipstick rim
yell down at strangers
Arvin faces Birdland
hey lady light look up & shine
no eyes for food
eyes for your lady fish
gold glass bottom
sky closed down
three little words

down below blue serge dungeons
deeper than smashed used-up oceans
office speak they spoke
everyone's in court
under arrest thrown in the hole
Bing & Bob do little claps
gray boys buzz on
won't be Uncle Remus Tom or Sam
no eyes
instead Watts eyes for poundcake
have another helping

one long for you
two long for me
wait for left people
who's a needle dancer
plays eyes shut
forehead wants to
thud ivories like me
an oxford gray that gray boys
hold as one of theirs
while he cops a mask
Big Chief blood fries their whys
but keeps toes tapping
what did I do to be so black & blue

pp

this heart of mine
motion moves devotion
out into air for all to share
its moment uplifted elevated
no words but bulging eyes
size it all up in one
sweet open end solo
sews up the end of time
extend it forever

all of me in you & me
when we dream as one
in the chase the kid on trumpet
stumbles into beauty
we hold up his flight
support the moment
society's made new for you

how to swing uplift's road
brass surround & Bill's sound
between air & ride cymbal
nimble splash the world's greatest
rhythm section if they asked me
I could write a book

blues at the bottom blues at top
I'm not a repeater pencil
don't like a whole lotta noise
no goddamn way
am looking for something soft
a little puff lady puts on her pussy
when she cleans up
it's got to be sweetness
soft eyes for me

waiting around for vanishment
banished at birth to the skin game
say man slip me some skin
graft my gray
in street beat shuffle vanishing act
facts all wrong in the obit
dig
born then gigs
then how sad then Lady Day
then more sad then blue turning gray
then all of me I can't get started
you're supposed to slip through walls
movie ghost style into another unreal
out of sight & slip on gripless banana peel
slaps edge trap shut on the ledge
I pray alone I play & wail
without you or me messing up the changes
still a stranger in my heartbeat at medium tempo

justice & just us
red dog in sax case
fuck you fuck me
where's your poundcake
lady peaches & cream
sing me song

I'm okay man I don't feel a draft
got a home in Long Island where the grass is green

pennies from heaven
review the books
I never really made it
all the other ladies
play like me
all the ladies come to hear me
but make all the money
mean to me

I give they take
they make it & I break down
into spit corroded brass
asleep in my green
horn-net on the hotel room bed

they salute me from the street
the ladies on slick feet walk
backward and forwards at the same time
eyes on all sides of their heads

dig
I'm always loosening spaces
laying out
my three little rhythms & me
happiness

don't like a whole lotta noise
eight changes where there oughta be two
ladies take it & run it back wrong
but cop bread in fistfulls
too much cement in spaces
no eyes for too much when enough's the truth

he's an old junky
he's an old funky funking & all that shit

no shit
no shit in my nose
nothing
I'll drink & smoke
ivy-divy

seeing's believing & hearing's a bitch
all the physicians come to hear the musicians

chill not cool what's in core
deep day or night marrow
edge out between sets
at dawn a passing slice
cuts through blues & empty beds
wind fuss brittle curtains
stir cigarette haze

all the ladies come to see me but
Stan gets the money
you dig

Johnny Deathbed
buries us deep & ripe for worm chow
each afterwards mulch filled with
new names engorged fat to busting
got-to-eat their way out
don't be nervous don't be scared
don't play eight changes when
there oughta be two

just two ladies sitting on a cup
one fell in & the other stood up
& walked out the door down stairs
back into Birdland for some suede cat
grayer than London to get done once more

coming back for more of the same pain
feels so good like I knew it would
it's very clear our love is here to stay
slip between sets your parting shot
hot slot tight behind the screen
cats pass by on their way to the can

in & out of the groove
sparkle plenty
big eyes between us all

no eyes in the jungle you dig
monkeys fill unreal green trees
fanged tiger rage
pounce on uncool pith helmet
haul souvenir baskets on bent back for Bwana
camera crew takes all they can
camp behind nets on julep nod
rusting Rolexes
& upstairs are scribbled stars

no eyes for uptown jungle jams
flat brown belly
rub against rippled black belly for gray
jerkoff pleasure slave block pussy fancy
rhythm section chains offbeat & slide
trombone growl humps
wa-wa trumpets probe ceiling
splashed with radium stars

no eyes for Africa or ancestral wigwams
mixing it up gumbo ya ya hybrid stew whose
blues bluer than blue
tapshoe faster than a drum riff
shoot down ten new cats on line
waiting to sit in & mix it up
it's all a mix up

I'm not the one you're looking for
not the one you're looking at

no eyes to see you
be a blind cat
like Art who sees all 88 stars
thrown back into place in space
shine us all on
who play in light
eyes roll back
inside the inside

no eyes but cradle your unseeing head
in music hands
listen for breath which won't come
we're on deathbed row
Johnny's cut out
got you in his sack
long gone

was it because we was slaves we was ladies
we danced for you
played your war horns
that you corked up to play us back
the Young family band in tents
real minstrels never had a chance

us ladies never black enough for your high white
that cuts nuts off with one hand
yanks out elephant tusks with the other
were we supposed to be what you weren't
why was it our fault
was it we was slaves
doing shit you daren't touch
puff-up cloud pillows
so close to heaven
who are you in gray white empty skin page
angry at night we wear in skin game
skin shame you mark & mock as mystery
tried on & cast off
for a moment
ooh
so cool & free of white weight
poor doves smash before flight

stretch & shrink while music from below
rises up through open Arvin window
sing one long raggedy song whose
rooftop pigeons bebop babble backbeat
mitten sounds mate for life

I was a kid in beat of open end days
the band rehearsed in the livingroom or in a tent
where tophat shamans begat blown glass bottles
of elixirs nostrums cure-all fix-all green or cherry red
hangover juice could hit limits before crashing
passage into death's shadow plays & shit all over
        your
head in a bowl
heave hallelujah

I was a kid in offbeat Baptist exaltation
hug everybody lift them upwards
beyond dust into big picture eternity
if you couldn't hear it
it wasn't music
it wasn't spirit

sad old cat in a flat hat no longer a kid
who reads the notes even when they dance away

it was smoothness man
no knots
great spreads of possible
infinite ease & clearness
through brasswork maze & leaky pads

amazing breath & space gone
each second it works its way
out an instant ghost

---

constitutional psychopathic state
manifested by drug addiction
(marijuana, barbiturates)
chronic alcoholism
& nomadism

eyes for bells & sweet dreams
in & out of nowhere bus stop town
drift on a reed
dread nothing but you'll never know
just how much I love you

sheik of Araby on a spread of sand going on
        indefinitely
snakecharm cactus into rose gardens
three little word blossoms sex red
fuzzy yellow dot-dot-dash misty pistils

oh say can you see PFC Young in KP bughouse band
uncoiled skins float in wet tubs

wander through blues & woe &
don't the moon look lonesome shining through the
        trees
sliced & dialed dealt & thrown on the table
a fan of fate the fat AWOL cat

reads like a book writ by star blotted clouds
chunky angels & red hot devils stir the stew

grays & ofays stoke a furnace
melt down Conns & Selmers into
honey poured ingots of eyes
spoons Tambo washboards his chest
in blaze of gold tonk
PFC cap in hand scout a shaded spot
anywhere in limitless seeking oasis
where the players are always ready

moon scimitar masonry
stitched into cat's fez opens a rude door
into courtyard dazzle garden
Jo Jones brushes blur in figtree shade
brass bowl cornucopia
brilliant outgush eye ache
water beaded fruits spill out onto white linen
Freddie Green sips thick black coffee out of tiny
            white cup
Basie puff puff hookah hooked into Buck's horn
cloudy ladies wait for the downbeat

solo out into smoke woven void
lonely not alone sweet & lovely Lester leap in
yellow ripple jade pool plunge her beige body
a fish in deckled light chips arise
with eyes & hands me a mouthpiece to suck in
            sunrise

Quasimodo bells tinkle uncorked navel of universe
no wavering in arising together a clatter of rainfall
spritzes the rest of the band in palm tree oasis

sheiks of make believe on funky hilly camels
clop over endless desert going everywhere &
        nowhere

when I was alone I always moved
into the brain fuck flower grew roots
choked off air its blossoms blinding me

when I was with you or her or any other lady
I was alone & moving in my mind
gets dark & fuck flower abundant
skull fills with irrepressible growth
blocks light but unlocks song sounds
riff glide think on the balls
of your suede shoes
work through blues changes

if I was a leper would I be more alone
in your body's shadow

nobody noticed where I sat or stood with my horn
backstage downstairs in the tan room painted
        nicotine
a jar of joints
offered to ladies all & one
we inhale
hold it down & exhale carillons
millions of trail maps
straight lines spiral loops up & down the ether
rewinds chimes to new cosmo riffs in

light renewing righteousness
laughter's logic kicks in

brother we're all alone here even when we're
     together
except when we give it up & come to each other's aid
music making for the unknown is all we know
sister solitary in the very act
fuck flower lady sister
solo nomad rumples bedsheets
off duty hotel dick at keyhole rocks off
sweet & isolate lovely other
what did I do
to be so black & blue

seeing's believing hearing's a bitch
woke up this morning ten feet underground
camels over my face buried in sand
& drop camel kaka as they bobble
sheik of Birdland on my funky steed
heads out of nowhere
everywhere the page stretches in any direction
can't get started point me anywhere
dig it
equal emptiness space
nothing signifies something mystifies
hemorrhoid sore atop carpet haired creature
blow lonely solos lost dust saliva
dries to powder coughed into her ear
spill chilled white wine over music
time blurs notes melt memory dissolves
what do I want isn't what you want
coming to table one night after night
w/ your ladies & your buddies to have it
happen as it happened it can't happen
that way ever again & you're stuck
in anger w/ what keeps moving beyond you
you're stuck

yeh it's also a gig
you know
something you got to be at
if you want the bread

my chronics part of chronos
day & night get carved up
into rite & wrong habits
guy next door's got his TV on
day & night
how much can you watch
how much can you see
black & white shit
fry in lights on Lady
me & old cats
do blues for dot watchers
nobody doesn't have some habit
rubbing rabbit's foot
shoot smack grab a taste a toke

chronics have a rhythm
falls into place
measured
so many bars
fill up pages
beginners transcribe my solos
do it by ear
do it by pen
let it play back all you know
all of me why not take all of me

afternoon session for Lady
smoke get ready for cats behind glass
pulling levers watch dials eraphones
yeah I meant ear-phones but dig
you always hear where you are
or where you were
the music keeps you in time

cats amble in
clock second-hand's a razor
slicing up numbers
"take one" barks producer behind glass
walls thick as death as impenetrable
our moments coil through wires
scratched into shellac
us ghosts just you just me
no little chaps

this ain't a molly trolley
they're taking it away
into wires behind glass
gray boys smoke & snap
their fingers any which way
whisper off-mike

low grade back up trio fakes it &
tries to make it
another audition for a paying crowd
crows & pigeons fight for crumbs
no flight in this joint
uphill work
watch the old guy play your dreams

in the movie he reaches up from the gutter
for one last high note
shatters bottles & glasses in rows behind the bar
go man go
have another shot

hit the edge & then
slip off the ledge without a sound
into bottomless applause pit
where clawed gimmes jimmy your brain
drain your soul & hang you up in the closet
mothball reek wreck & tamed empty
see what I mean

we be whores
get out there to bump the honk
granzstand it for grogged pitbulls
they bark their burp say
go man go
no matter what you play
sweet things or funk bucket
they want meat & spines
torn out sent flying
where they can't imagine
& never get to & stay angry
no matter what

what losers those johns

always looking for something soft
bury me in cashmere
a buzz so fine time backs off

soft in the sound of Jo or Al Hibbler
soft eyes for little puff
soft puff muff never enough
gift me softly get me going
out in softness of your eyes
sounds surround our play
we improvise the ever same
inside each other alone together

not for unaware squares in chairs
off synch seals bark at bait
just for you
ladies in silk of digging
in nylon of receiving
in warm milk of forgiveness & acceptance
but finally really
just me just you
can't you see I can't give you
anything but love

c ♪

let's review the books
what adds up
all those other ladies play like me
make all the money
they all come to hear me
but I don't make their money
& Johnny Deathbed out the corner of my eye
gives me shit about immortality is what you die for
what's it worth sonny boy
when I don't have copies of my own
records to spin on the phono
lights down below
shine back on your face in shadows above me
morning storm of pain & sweet
release but fuck what do I realize
dumb eyes
no eyes

⌒

ff

I can't I don't play like that anymore
I play different, I live different
now is later, that was then
we change, move on

me myself & I dies off stage
turn the page back into dark
someone turns the lights on
them there eyes can't get me started
parting there'll be some changes made
tell the story

I'm a ghost of chance & changes
too marvelous for words

Herschel Evans taps his forehead
there's things going on up there, man
some of you guys are all belly
it's all about breath & air
how you split pads down the center
twin columns
two registers of breath
circle up air spine & comes out voice

eyes for the gig but
how does the bread smell

ghost don't stand a ghost of chance
red ghost w/ gold skin & green eyes don't know
what time it was taking a chance on love

watch those draughts that draft
Von Hangman's here
along w/ Johnny Deathbed
& Lady Scythe
writes me in her book

stoke that smoke & hit that gin
basic training hup two three four
Private 39729502
Psycho nomad drug addict juicer
tote that barge & do that time
on my hands whose people play pretty
right or left of just you just me

o　　o　　o

ghost of a phrase
E flat A flat E flat D flat
over G7 chord

o　　o　　o

Selmer Balanced Action tenor

they come for something else
JATP honk honk w/ Flip
tenors locked in hype
people get gassed
$50,000 the first year
not bad for being good

takes two to tango two to tangle
drop your drawers girl
Oscar's left & right people
cover ivory ear loops
who knew me
how was I known
what's left
fat from not eating
black porkpie hat shades green eyes
puff & taste
bells
pops

how slow did it go
last night she walked out
before it began

with no place else to go
turn the phono on
sip & listen
where or when

how they tell it
tell the story
there's a glisten I listen for

stuff inside
folds into layers of more stuff
& the photo got it right
at bed's edge
stunned Prez scopes dim angel
rosining a bow

how slow does it go
as long as it takes
to work itself through
to close it all down

clothe it in another light
eyes & bells
bells & eyes

Prez in Paris sips pernod
chimes like boo
loose in milky green
digs the scene
everybody knows his work
like Picasso or Leonardo
it's almost like being in love
city of love lights
sweet twisty streets
petals flutter down on
porkpie hat crown

one awakes knowing sleep's forever
a blue neon wind gets through cracks
a low watt bulb on the table means you're able
to shut your eyes & read the book of life
& hear audience roar oceans beyond
voices no longer avoid the erased face
in the mirror doesn't look back anymore
got a key to the door & the lobby's a slow show
everybody knows sleep's forever
newsguy takes bets on the side
how long before Prez slides out of the picture

all the way in it
enormous solo
lasts less than a minute
what can I say

when you fall into heaven do you land
on a spot where wandering stops
when you fall into paradise is it merely nice
like an awards ceremony or a device
to cut through grease & finally address
everything by its first name
equality a tapestry
gypsy fortune teller crystal globe
popped on shawl top tablecloth
author the next eternity on a rolled-out roadmap
where every rest stop is arresting compelling
heavenly sites are gold circles on a scroll
I roll with the road & flow with the going

when you check into heaven is it *carte blanche*
livre noir or neither nor just one open door
after another & you can choose any room
champagne in an ice bucket
nice flowers on the table
or tequila on a mantilla with a pile of limes &
rock salt salutes shot glass rim with vim & rigor
or overflowing bowls of chop suey
pink with jumbo shrimp
hugged by glistening greens & plump mushrooms
served by ladies in slit silk skirts
buttoned in jade & bowed in gold pouring
the best gin berries conceivable

believe it
sorrow cools it in nomad's land
& kisses long as spring & everybody
sings sweet like Lady can't you see

when you walk out the bronze revolving door
into floor after floor of better & better
no need for names like heaven or paradise
instead play nice for everyone throw delicate
flowers in warm showers of coming honey
into a choir of fine ladies playful & sunny
in room after room where you never see blue
it's all umber you dig it's all a play of pearls
sweet pink pussy lips blow three little words
into goose down swords
stabbed with arrows Cupid silks our loins with
Eros give up the weight & freight keeping us back

when you walk out of the picture no longer there
in a chair by a window or edge of a bed
everyone instead becomes memory in heaven
blow so cool club walls melt
hot chocolate over all the cats in ecstasy
dig a one & only
& keep it going like dervishes
in one blur of fur & skin wins the race
over & over again
when you disappear
fear disappears with you

when you leap into space beyond belief
free of it articulate able to say it all
who's there behind the door
Johnny Deathbed or Jesus Christ slicing
oranges & pears onto a white plate
passed my way as an invite to stay
when you say goodbye you're already
looking to say hello to anyone going along
a road of light like lava angels tapdance over
& out jim it's simply zipped & done
with wings & mirrors

was there too in hoodoo's doing
as a kid & old man to dig how
what's unseen sees & what sees is blind
& ears straw it to heart
parts hot curtains to love's hot
butter knife slices certainty
out of the picture into melody
you never see but always know

when the maestros come back on stage
to encore the impossible
I'm back in Woodville being born
August 27 1909

back being born through horn
on a road to anywhere
wherever they drop you off
man it's a gig

back being born
you could care for me
abandoned it stays prayerful
welcome wherever I am
except in mean rooms ruled by death

being born
back when news was still blues & you
a lady in dues waitingrooms
my love made up new lies for

being born adored then shown the door
to a map of snaky routes going straight
into just us never getting justice
sun gets nailed in soul
clamped into a fist
they hear you on a hard skid
poetry against bombast
push bodies
either way onto the dancefloor

born a seeing eyed dog
poke into your heat for love
for a taste in the waste of the rest of it
dogged when born for your love
taste outside air water shine
root for suck to test predawn warmth
& move to each slice
dice cut loose a wandering juicehead
not dead somewhat alive
still hip to your jive

busy being born
as many times as there are
choruses of *How High the Moon*

busy being born in my horn
you & the night & the music

busy cutting you loose
break cables disable all your moves

busy bleeding
seeding
receding sound decay
closing-up clatter
brass cymbal sizzle
last water circle glows
Jones tones grow

men pack up breath in cases
carried back to rooms
they can't sleep in

pack & unpack cases
where brass swans rest
in between gigs & sessions
on beds of crushed black or blood red velour

a salesman on the job
men pack & unpack cases
to anybody who'll listen
get the glisten gleam of need
let loose in music pitch & itch to be free
want it all in a box to open
break seal after seal
verify a good deal in utopia
dope in a sea of schemes
on a paperhat boat soak up
oilspill & spiel
as fast as they roll out lines
& pull you in

packup after a gig &
look around for anybody left
in the last note

dirty floors & doors locked until
tomorrow's grief
& borrowed chits keep me alive
one more day

oh pack it up old man
let young cats land on their feet
trash your past & praise you
master the moment
day breaks & coffee gets cold
outside light knifes beauty
pay bills dust on sills
owe dues
sing blues old man
younger than most

pack it in jim the job's done
nobody around to imagine
what music made of you & me
stale leftover smoke & unwashed
glasses stacked in a bar sink

kiddies come to check how it's done
sneak out to try it down the block

I blow for a company
named after a flyingcarpet
got a wife & kids
don't mind the waterfall
can't stand the mustard

pack it in jim the job's done
everybody's back home sleeping alone
radium clockface shines on anxious
dreamers snug in a house blues paid for
when I'm late
doors double-locked
crash elsewhere
daylight stares back
& tacks my eyes shut

where do nomads go
when no man knows your name
alone in nowhere's nowhere
hot metals in the case burn your hand
sand shifts to stand on
no oasis but play in shade
where spooks in gowns
float over palmtrees
go Prez go & camels
sleep standing up

where do nomads go in No Man's Land
land's end sea carries sheet music
out to no sense horizons
float wherever it goes into
ukulele sunset yodel *Amazing Grace*
Precious Lord
Georgia Tom wrote the myth of future
for folks with phonographs
a round paradise around 78 rpm mph
pure spiral mechanism of messiah spirit
through cosmic air column from heaven
through earth to hell
icebergs melt down into honey streams
release torment
set free
Precious Lord take my nomad hand
to someone's promised land

set me up in the best band anyone can imagine
anywhere
& all will hear the call & respond
& all will arise

eyes to arise through beauty's clouds
cast off gabardine shrouds

Johnny Deathbed blows cool holes
through damaged souls
all his axe's gold fools & corrodes in your hand
& the band lays stiff in brass handled death ships
sails of wailing widows
can't lift death weight
whitegloved pallbearers strut the load
before death flattens them
turned inside out into ever constant food

forever marble eyes see nothing
see sky tombstones spread
out like tract homes
tracheotomies
in the middle of fucking nowhere

rifle & pack sir
don't want anything after a taste
don't do nothing
don't care to blow my horn
don't care to be around anybody

Lester the moocher
sponges off buddies
to keep on the move
play here & there all busted up
& down the street
pups line up to hear & ditto

fatal art bops back
cats in between notes meet
tone beats stoned flats diminish
can't finish upwing it swing it new
blues blast speed show tunes
them/us handkerchief over pads
in dark caves berets Euro Islam
scat attack plantation crap
can't get started all of me
a mystery can't you see
w/ no eyes but to be
one dot beyond seeing

long tongues scrape out the briar patch
wraps around fool lungs
fake hair covers up real terror
back luck motherfuckers
stuck where your pecker glues
blues down on brass keys
ain't no shit to be shit
dig
whether you dig or not
it catches up to you
long tongues chews your shadow up
spits it back as buckshot
duck motherfucker
time's up

Jo's broken rhythms
Sweets' Harmon buckeye mute
mistakes sound good but
good's no mistake
let's gas them wannabes
let's please ourselves
honeybees hiving not jiving
hit it Doc let's do blues

In a little Spanish town
Señor Prez parks his fez &
sips margaritas through pink straws
jaws w/ señoritas & munches
toastitos dipped in salsa suprema
tongue tip burns brain
limes & salts & worm fuel aslant
on wicker bar stool in sombrero
tinkle multicolored wool bells
nobody sells nothing & a chick
at the other end starts singing
I guess I'll have to change my plan

some gonzo caballero wrapped in
banderillas goes loco from this year's kisses
shoots out a chandelier
glass snow over everyone
mariachis strike up somebody loves me
a cool brass breeze heats up dance
& out of the woods come Zapatistas
& tourists flourish in exalt
in a mist remove ski masks & shades
can't we be friends at another end
happy or otherwise

in a world everyone thought they knew
dancing through it

blues 'n' bells
imagine me imagine you
these foolish things remind me of Doc Cloud
I die on Friday the 13th 1959
I found a new baby
$500 in traveler's checks
wait for nobody but me
& you're too marvelous for words

jammin' the blues Gjon
froze frames & drapes
move still into a reel
smoky black & white
head tilted to one side
accommodate the 45 degree
twist of his mouthpiece

don't stand a ghost of a chance
slicked up spook
from jook joint jive
sharkskin musky sweat
spermlet salt tip sour
cut up blade hand
glide onto bandstand
these foolish things haunt
what your hair covers up

not jam sessions KC style but
gladiator galas for ofays
ache to get down or be seals
bark & clap clap
go go go to any noise
but tub thumpers get thumbs up

Hollywood fantasy
hover between shades
sparks & sharks
chew heat's beat
energize thighs
inside protein circles
explode eyes
expel skin
take it home
folklore it
gossip or
let it alone

jaws close & lips form
an airtight seal on a sliver
of cane & wedge of metal
or plastic becomes voice
diaphragm pushes lungs &

expelled air vibrates reed
whose moves vibrates teeth
mouth sinuses

Von Hangman's here
in shit stained KKK sheets
knife picks teeth
wants my grief
thief'll rip my eyes out
scandalize my name
when I dance wrong
to the cool
broke blue mouth

to die on a tree of life's a riddle
Von Hangman's been hanging
peoples before & after I was born

Von Hangman drags bones
top a slick black pony
snorts fire spark confetti
hoofs do dainty tapdance on copper sheets
blood path maps journey

Von Hangman's got B-movie eyes
battery-run red lights roll up into
gold cave brain skull
scrolls lists of cats
& chicks his trick book

crows hook to his shoulders
Von Hangman counts each crop
with cool eye & smug remove
caw caw
always more always more

Von Hangman's a hungry sucker
who never worries about more helpings

⌒

they say my work was introspective
reflective of inner pain & no gain
a juice life lost to unspecified grief
w/out relief

tic critics get under your skin

indecisive triplet decorations
shuffle in lower register
a grainy tone
loose sounds
vibrato at end of phrases
quivering taut string
softer reed
vulnerable & deep beyond belief

1955 nervous breakdown
gloom weights drown
stone clown glub glub into deep diver
w/out rival only copycats
on gold strings enter
spotlight's ring
fame claims you
mint coin get gelt man
no bullshit plaque
no free lessons
sessions for the love of it
shit
no eyes for that
I'm blindfolded in laughing barrel's bottom
suck up breath of dead slave laughter
into blues 'n' bells

who am I if not a riddle
riffed by some stone Sphinx
in the middle of another jive desert
unpeels exodus sun pours
honey back into a hive of horns

shit was it ever as
good as it felt

was I there
were you?

---

don't want to play w/ no highschool kids
kiddies don't groove me
no eyes
need guys who know
enough to cause doubt & art
to blow a fuse

𝄐

man am I blue
out there
wigged on you
& you already out the door
wear the wrong suit & dumb shoes

man am I blue out here
notes but no script
grays rustle my sound w/ wire
reel wheel eyes to get it all
down & done
in the cheat book

man in blue
paid his dues
ain't through
who the fuck are you
cop my free stuff
all my bad luck

scuffed at heels
aslant blue man glides on stage
as in days gone
Hollywood soundstage cats
puff smoke haze
for Mili's 35 millimeter

man sings blues to you
all day & ready for nightlight
fight w/ sweet heat & jive meat
part thighs w/ honey sweet lies
salt retreats
know it all but
no eyes no lies no shit

"a night person
he *entered* the evening"
sticks & bones jazz sage
plastic reed fries up buzz
come rain or come shine
'54 gloom ramshackle quaver
tear drops condense around
spine's heart Bellevue bound
replace gin w/ wine
space out
eat some food to fill empty
new gigs w/ young cats
spin 'em back to where it's at
what art does jim
parts the peepshow veil

Doc Cloud
says I'm talking sense now
it's okay to bon voyage to Paris
ah Doc Cloud billows gray white lace fluff
glides o'er deep torque turquoise summer skies
merci merci at Blue Note & gin some
Doctor Cloud I presume I didn't know
what time it was & I can't get started

French cats w/ Klook time chickyboom
cover the waterfront in Indiana lady
be good where sea pulls away
in Paree man cats statue you
wreathe your bean w/ laurels
on gold scrolled marble base

pity to die in love's city of light
instead go home alone
to dead end Alvin &
end dead Friday the 13th
chair by window
drink between heaves
lay down & sleep
Broadway lights ding on & on
& wake ripped
fingertips move to pads

make mouth into horn embouchure
fall back
fall in fall out
die

bulls come in scan anything of value
to cover hotel bill
$500 in traveler's checks
wallet ring
worn funky Selmer
Balanced Action tenor

buried in Evergreen Cemetery
in Queens w/ all the other ladies

⌒

ladies above below go where God moves you
through worn tunnel
another pile-up of souls
downpour sequin essences
gleam arc moves sheathed in feathers
petal papered dazzle overhead lights
beauty fury taps counterpoint on ivory toggles
kliegs snap out ghost tableaux
gold shrine shrouds
Frankie & Jimmy tell stories on C-melody
Yard's got eyes for everything on his plate

brass knights rage on stage
honk smash & clank horn clash
storm against roaring grays
I cut your throat all due respect
whirlwind slams out
Lady Be Good choruses

ah kiddies be so beyond invisible
masked w/ jive hungry to survive
out cool out hot out out
please you & sucker punch you
soon as the light turns green

east of the sun west of the moon

be bop don't stop me
I play different I live different
this is later that was then
we change we move on

apostles of lowdown clarinet slur
stately march for gone gate spirit
breath through horns in formation
down Death nation's narrow avenue
drum rolls off to umph the trump
& strum soul into a new world
lost you find me in black & white
photograph shuffle of album covers
liner note laurels silk band
around porkpie hat
smoke halo let me go
don't hang me in your livingroom

ff

it was so short-lived it hardly counts
the second Mrs Young
was white & married Lester
in California maybe in 1943
bore him two children

⌒

all the years of white mystery
I sought mastery over brass & breath
a history you don't conceal its real
chest breaking hammers of nigger
gelded welded mouth full of death
what did I do to be so black & blue

we never rehearsed anything
he never said anything
about how I should play
I guess he was satisfied
I kept the job
Lester never played more than three
choruses on anything
it was very unusual
if he played four
there were times
when I wanted him to play more
but he wouldn't
he always left you
wanting more
rather than play all night
until you got tired of hearing him

everybody w/ their fucking memories
billboards Burma Shave clutter got in the way
of what was really happening
only once & only forever gone

if Prez's kiddies were here now
they'd *know* what to do

like WB Prez died at 50

feel a draft
a mocha surface
their eyes coldly decode

feel a draft
eye knife peels skin
into blood

feel a draft on lifeboat
ration out black meat to feed folks

feel a draft in Cafe Society
hangman's knotted silk tie
Cartier gold watchband garrote

feel a draft between day & night
light they shine into my room
making sure I'm asleep

feel a draft on a plane going to Spain
tourist wrist twists its KKK knot
around an imagined wreck

feel a passing glance draft

bounce off storewindow mirrors
signals terror
turn away as if we weren't anywhere to be seen
but imagined everywhere

feel a draft pick up short change wage
from sports who traffic in jazz slaves
on a stage too small for shadows
crawl away out the back door

feel a draft on a raft the three of us
two grays & guess who

feel a draft coming down
before badge buddies ask questions
no answer's right

feel a draft on the upswing
hit glass they watch me through

⌒

it's not tragic jack
it's facts made bells
rolled into chime smoked carillons
a million bucks can't touch

tell your story know the lyrics
it's all song no matter how wrong
the facts or how high the moon

know where you're going
where you're coming from

no way not to pay

play what stays

yesterdays

perfunctory respect
& too many musicians merely
seemed to suffer him

he'd lost weight
his clothes draped his frame
couldn't waste time & money
being a fashion plate

he was a night person
he *entered* the evening
even the quantity of his words
increased as daylight decreased

enter night through door veils
hot silk skin sear your fine brown frame
move into star seeded deep black back
streets & doors where parquet floors store
grunge angles of careless time

it's the dark talking shade talk
crazy spook looks ahead & behind
everywhere blind to dividing lines

Doc Cloud don't talk loud
don't talk shroud

Prez accepts it beautifully
cuts the cake drinks champagne
tilts down to wilted figs
& digging stop-time wigs

Pierre & Rene at Blue Note
after 3 weeks strength goes
stomach pains
too weak to un-bed
instead hail a cab to Orly
vomit blood in coffin head
Friday the 13th 1959

cab to Arvin chair by window
drink steadily readily headily
wake abrupt moving fingers
form embouchure mouth
fall back roll eyes beyond & die

they took everything of value
to pay hotel bill

$500 traveler's checks
wallet, ring & Selmer
Balanced Action tenor saxophone

boxed & bottomed
Evergreen Cemetery in Queens
Doc Cloud heard it on the car radio

they want every negro
to be an Uncle Tom
or Uncle Remus
or Uncle Sam
& I can't make it

boxed & placed in soil
a seedling all used up

⌢

B flat Blues from DC man
flat out the ride leap
onto/into nada
move too fast
too many chancy changes
few do that hoodoo more than you do
blow freaky around chord stacks
young cats flutter ruffle shuffle magic act
cards arc into air into place
into edgeless unopened deck
man that's fool's gold

all my love is all I've got for you
& the night & the music
no words but bells but
lyrics outside explaining
you wrap your soul inside of
a shimmer silk glove fits like a rubber
heats up love why not take all of me

last gasp last pass through white plastic inlay
       mouthpiece
Ebonite Brilhart Ebolin
in the 402 a metal mouthpiece by Otto Link
what do you think
what's left of breath
drink gin out of teacup wreathed
w/ handpainted flowers
though April showers leaky pads
Fine & Mellow TV red eye allows one chorus
it's all there & there too in opening clarinet of
They Can't Take That Away from Me 1958
w/ Roy & Sweets & Norman at the board

everybody around
nobody's gone
sound vapors
always in the air
replay to this day
vanishing act
sorry I couldn't stay
was there when it counted

doodle & noodle
before the door
cuts light off
it gets
not only mysterious
but serious

c

it's not dying or crying
or blues
it's the work of getting it right
in a moment
no cornball monument
just a statement of who where
when it was what

discs & photos
separate & divide me
from my art
I am imagined
I remain unknown

another New Year's gig in pit of
potted jazzers deep into confetti

sweep up is what creeps do
cool cats sleep

what's cool isn't what you drink
drape or shade or lay back on
what's outside ain't it either

if you ask you don't know
if you know you don't ask
it's how
not what

worn wise
sad glad
bad but good
truth lays out
alive but dead
feed her roots

Lester leaps in
on curved arch
shaving a reed

young cats
grays or not
either way
put too much dressing on the salad

it's fight for your life
till death do we part
you got it made but
they take advantage of me
the same all over
can't take that bull*shit*
you dig
it's all bull*shit*
& it's rough out here
but I'm enjoying myself
up here by myself

to get away from all that shit
& things & I ain't got a quarter
but I don't walk around sighing blues
'cause my old lady'll take care of me
so fuck it

what people do
man
is so obvious
what the fuck I give a fuck what you do
what he do
what he does

what nobody do
is nobody's business

he's an old junky
old funky
old fucky
all I do is smoke New Orleans cigarettes
that's perfect
no snit
no shit in my nose
nothing
I drink & smoke
that's all
that's that

I stay by myself so
how the fuck do you know
anything about me?

"Prez, I thought you were dead"
I'm more alive than you are
give me my three little rhythms & me
a little puff a lady puts on her pussy when
she cleans up & shit like that
soft eyes for me

I can't *stand* no loud shit
you dig
& bitches come in New York

& trumpets scream & shit
& bitches put their fingers in their ears
you know
it's got to be sweetness, man
you dig
sweetness can be funky filthy or anything
but which part do *you* want?
the funkies or the sweet?
shit
what am I talking about?

when I get back I got
bass violin two cellos a viola
& a French horn
see what I mean?
& three rhythms
you know what goes with that

Norman Granz never did let *me*
make a record with no strings
Yardbird made millions of records
with strings & things

what he do—what he doesn't—
is nobody's business

for all we know
we may never meet again

Came to NY in '34 w/ Henderson
& Lady taught me the city
which way to go
where everything's shitty
where it's pretty
you dig

don't put that weight on me
I know what I do

the Apple's rotten
falls apart to touch
& now I'm done

lost or found we're still
mid passage iron tied & timed
by work's whips cut by
vicious & ambitious grays
brother salt decays our tropical ark
wood sepulcher
long before Virginia let us in

Lester's insouciance was cool
a word that's lost all coolness
laidbackness
its power to defuse & confuse
diffused in Netscape blips & MTV
hip hop flip flop meager wages
surface glare & glide
slide easy digital tic toc
cool clock cool time
everything's so fucking cool
bodies float up on vicious poolside pane
shot through fiberoptic hairstrands
Prez adrift saunters off the bandstand
across the street in a reet
buzz of blue serge words

cool wasn't home ache
trayf plastic schlock
giddy banal kitsch

backwards it's almost "look"
eyes to see each immense detail
now flat as plywood

profuse confusion obliterates
apologies or denials

everything's cool

a hiccup
a tic stuck in the loop
a splinter of retrieval already lost

"here I go again
falling in love again"

go Prez
fall into love again
in the spin again
loving the spin I'm in
on downtown bus
white highschool kids say cool
young dulls say cool
Willie the Penguin
Joe Camel's pa says
Smoke Kools
it's all one linked tanka
up in smoke

1947 Town Hall concert
Lester scats count-down to each tune
a soft high hip flutey
zoot suitey voice
1944 Bebop's eve
Dickey Wells wails between tones
like Dolphy's free careening or
Monk's sliding handkerchief dance

no eyes roll back into dark skull cave
exit door through backyard's tall grass
dark as molasses in thick pre-tornado stop
before it all hits

how can you refuse the blues
what's to lose
close the door when you leave

believe what you enter or
you're seized in impossibility
frozen between neither nor

you can't join the throng
until you write your song

the song is you
I hear music everywhere you are

you are my lucky star
& the night & the music

to go you got to know the words

to go you got to know
you got to go to know the words

you fall into the shawl of familiar
grandpa on a backlot porch

you gotta look back w/ remorse
for kicks & fixes & routines

you wanna be cuddly
an anthem caught by
blue lens glaze on vapory scenes

your anger & rage soak out
into a page of three-color sheet-fed gravure

your blood a syrup on blind white ice
cream skyscrapers reach up to pink lips

your blues a glue antiquarians prize

your cool a fool's gold reconfigured
by lesser & lesser players & poseurs

your suave enigma style display
conceals deep empire

your broke & battered shatter
your moviestar decay

what is imagined
isn't what's played

what's played
is beyond imagining
who's the fading photo

why does everyone die
just
when we got to know each other

all of me why not
take all of me

⌢

if exhaustion were an ocean
I'd dive in head first
& forget how to swim

down to the deepest deep
creep along bottom's bottom
& sleep w/out dreaming

turn blue in salt cold
shrink old prune gray
water filled folds pop open
on sunny days

no more sweet or sour
just hour after hour of no time
is nobody's time w/ nobody around
to keep time

if misery were the sea
& blues were sky
I'd still sink & fly
& cry w/out anyone
being around to spy
on Prez & say shit

the suit fits
the wood fits
the earth fits
dark fits
worms fit right in
& out & who's to know
who's blowing elsewhere
who cares

if blues were shoes
I'd walk a million miles
& still not be through
my map of traps

to run changes is not my game
chords afford hills I climb
in time to sing a song lambs lap up
& love sap fills the meter w/ sweet
hearts no glass fills

paradiddle tap delicacy
clicketyclack on glass bridge
over skin abyss drum
of slaves stretched
beyond break &
beyond kiss

if lips were song

I'd never go wrong
& stay stuck on your mouth
breath to mine in a circle of fifths

if blues were shoes
I'd be barefoot before I start
walking in or out of
your life

if blues were news
the dailies would take eternity
to get through

when I go I go there without you
through back door
blue light blink exit
out of frame tilted
solo in transit

just a gigolo a photograph
an 8 x 10 print a postage stamp
passport ID
out the door into night

what I saw & you saw
never the same
not even close
where I looked in

you looked out
saw only skin

was light for a colored man
was colored for a light man
nobody wins the skin game

bells bells bells
smoke a carillon
thanks a million
high beam eyes
can't see nothing but
atoms & ladies
move through
cloud shadow snacks
spines of light on shades
slides of reverie

in Speed Graphic clubs
booths filled with suits & skirts
ashtrays & shot glasses
washed in flash
through time into
shutter's petals

if snaps were real
nothing'd get anywhere
if past was future's fingerprint

love'd go nowhere
& if each note froze before it went
there'd be nowhere to go
if you is or you ain't my baby
I'd still blow words you couldn't hear

⌒

Lester led the band with his eyes
he hardly said anything except
hey baby or you know

Ding-dong
hello goodbye
bells ring
when eyes see

in '42
in L.A.
Nat Cole
Red Callander
& Prez do
Tea for Two

breathless Lester
deathless

not brushes but
acetate fluster
sizzles digital

Bean & Byas did wood
Prez does air
Bean & Byas push it
Prez lets it

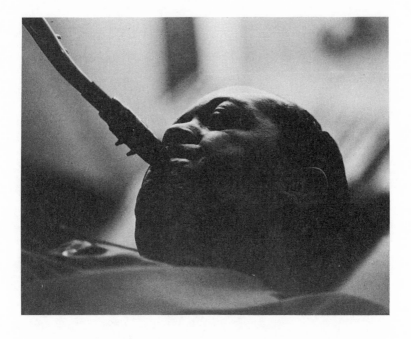

what's delicate
inviolate
rejects bruise
accepts blues

Bird learned from me
from Trumbauer's C-melody
& Dorsey's alto

pilfer from source
to become source

skin's secondary

⌒

asked me who I was
who they were
why we were
how I did it
who I got it from
what's the secret
I told them everything
& they heard nothing

born 1909 died in '59
it's '98
you'd be 80
on jazz cruise ship
a hunger artist
bypass the clam dip
go for distilled curl
a Filipino pours into
extra deep shot glass
knees push against leatherette
bar puff facade

elders scarf up all-you-can-eat
buffet at captain's table
Berklee kids set up gear
hey where's the chick singer

28 viii 97
Richmond
California

Printed May 2000 in Santa Barbara &
Ann Arbor for the Black Sparrow Press by
Mackintosh Typography & Edwards Brothers Inc.
Text set in Sabon and Sonata by Words Worth.
Design by Barbara Martin.
This first edition is published in paper wrappers;
there are 200 hardcover trade copies;
100 hardcover copies have been numbered &
signed by the author; & 22 copies lettered A–V
have been handbound in boards by
Earle Gray, each with an original drawing
by David Meltzer.

◊

PHOTO: Frank Pedrick

DAVID MELTZER is the author of many books of poetry and has edited numerous thematic anthologies including *Birth: An Anthology of Ancient Texts Songs, Prayers, and Stories* (1981) and *Death: An Anthology of Texts, Songs, Charms, Prayers, and Stories* (1984). He edited two major and controversial anthologies of jazz writing, *Reading Jazz* (1996) and *Writing Jazz* (1999), published by Mercury House. He is currently assembling a revised and expanded version of *The San Francisco Poets* for City Lights due to be published in 2001. Some of his agit-smut fictions of the late '60s were reissued by Rhinoceros and Richard Kasak Books (*Orf, The Agency Trilogy*) and a newer rant, *Under*, was published in 1995 by Rhinoceros. Associated with the Beat movement or moment, Meltzer read poetry in San Francisco's Jazz Cellar in the late '50s (working with jazz maestros like Pony Poindexter and Leo Wright) and in the '60s fronted Serpent Power, a psychedelic band recorded by Vanguard and Capitol. He began teaching in the mid-'70s at San Francisco's Urban School (a private high school) and then spent four years teaching writing at Vacaville Prison. Meltzer is now on the faculty of New College of California in the MA program in Poetics. Books by Meltzer currently in print with Black Sparrow are *Arrows: Selected Poetry 1957–1992* (1994); *The Name: Selected Poetry, 1973–1983* (1984); and *Six* (1976).